Seeking Justice

Anti-Bias Learning: Social Justice in Action

By Emily Chiariello

21st Century
Junior Library

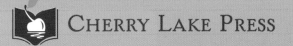

Published in the United States of America by Cherry Lake Publishing Group
Ann Arbor, Michigan
www.cherrylakepublishing.com

Developed with help from Learning for Justice, a project of the Southern Poverty Law Center. With special
thanks to Monita Bell and Hoyt Phillips.
Reading Adviser: Beth Walker Gambro, MS, Ed., Reading Consultant, Yorkville, IL

Photo Credits: © Rawpixel.com/Shutterstock.com, cover, 1, 18; © AnnGaysorn/Shutterstock.com, 4;
    © Rawpixel.com/Shutterstock.com, 6; © altanaka/Shutterstock.com, 8; © Paul Velgos/Shutterstock.com, 10;
    © Everett Collection/Shutterstock.com, 12; © Doug Lemke/Shutterstock.com, 14; © jumis/Shutterstock.
    com, 16; © Rena Schild/Shutterstock.com, 20

Library of Congress Cataloging-in-Publication Data has been filed and is available at catalog.loc.gov

Cherry Lake Publishing Group would like to acknowledge the work of the Partnership for 21st Century Learning,
a Network of Battelle for Kids. Please visit http://www.battelleforkids.org/networks/p21 for more information.

Printed in the United States of America
Corporate Graphics

CONTENTS

Fairness isn't that we all get the same things,
but that we all get the things we need.

Stereotypes

I know people in groups are not all the same.

"That's not fair!" Have you ever said those words? Maybe you meant that not everyone got the same thing. But **fairness** doesn't always mean that things are the same. Different people need different things. You wouldn't expect your little sister and your big brother to wear each other's shoes, would you? That wouldn't be fair. They would hardly be able to walk!

Stereotypes are usually based on how a person looks.
What might you not know about a person based on their looks?

Fairness means we don't give an **advantage** to some people over others. Another word to describe fairness is **justice**. Justice begins with treating people as unique individuals. It's unfair to think that all of the people in a group are the same as each other.

A **stereotype** is when we **assume** something about someone based on just one part of who they are. When we believe stereotypes about others, we are being **prejudiced**. We are judging someone before we know the truth about them. Stereotypes can cause feelings of prejudice either for that person or against them.

Saying what someone should or should not do because of their gender is wrong.

Maybe you've noticed some adults using **gender stereotypes**—ideas about what boys and girls *should* be like. But there are many ways to be a boy or a girl, both, or neither.

Even though many football players are men, a girl like Kendra can still love to play the game! And Kevin can grow up to be a beautiful ballet dancer, even though he is a boy and lots of ballet dancers are women or girls.

Create!

Create a classroom constitution with your teacher and classmates. What kinds of rules and agreements will you include to make sure the class is fair for everyone?

Taking more than your share of something is unfair.

What Is Unfairness?

I can describe what unfairness is.

When we seek justice, it means we are trying to make things fair. This means pointing out when things are unfair. Unfairness, or **injustice**, can happen in lots of ways.

One person can treat another person unfairly. Maybe you know someone who doesn't share nicely. Or you might know someone who cuts in line so they can get lunch first.

Black schools, like this high school, didn't have money
for enough teachers or school supplies.

Whole groups of people can also be treated unfairly. For many years in the United States, Black children and White children were forced to attend different schools. Black children experienced a lot of injustice just because of the color of their skin. Their schools did not get as much money as the schools for White children. But the schools for White children had more money to pay teachers and buy newer books and equipment. People fought for justice and made the government change the law to make things fairer.

Think!

Have you ever seen someone being bullied? Did you do anything? Did you say something? Think of what you might say or do to speak up the next time you see someone being treated unfairly.

European settlers unfairly claimed the land of North America
and tried to replace the people with a new society.

Unfairness Hurts

I know unfairness causes harm.

Being treated unfairly hurts. Injustice causes harm. Sometimes, the harm is small, but sometimes, it's big. The hurt feeling can be short, or it can last a long time.

Long ago, European **colonizers** stole the land that is North America from Native Americans who were already living here. The loss of their land and the struggles that followed caused great harm to Native American people. This harm continues today.

What might be some advantages to living in a city?
What about the disadvantages?

Advantages and Disadvantages

I understand that life is easier for some people and harder for others.

All people have certain advantages and **disadvantages** based on who they are and where they were born. Life is easier for some people and harder for others.

We don't get to choose where we are born. But where you are born will determine many of the experiences and **opportunities** you have.

Children everywhere should have the same chance to be safe and healthy.

Flora lives in a city apartment building that was built with unsafe materials. As a result, she and her siblings have **asthma** and other health problems. Her classmates who don't live in that building don't have the same problems.

If that sounds unfair to you, you're right. Seeking justice means making sure all children are born with a chance to be healthy.

C. T. Vivian worked alongside Martin Luther King Jr.
Find out more about him!

Justice Seekers

I know about the actions of people to make the world a fair place.

Throughout history, people and groups have worked to bring more justice and fairness to the world.

Some of those people are famous, like Dr. Martin Luther King Jr. But Dr. King had help from many brave people who you might not have heard of, like Bayard Rustin and Ella Baker.

How will you seek justice when you find unfairness in your life?

Ask Questions!

Talk to teachers and other adults in your life to learn about people who fought for justice throughout history. Ask questions to find out new things about people you haven't heard of before.

GLOSSARY

advantage (uhd-VAN-tij) something that helps or is useful to someone

assume (uh-SOOM) to believe something without asking or checking if it's true

asthma (az-MUH) a health condition that causes difficulty breathing

colonizers (KAH-luh-nye-zers) people who settle in an area and take control of it

disadvantages (diss-uhd-VAN-tij-ehz) things that make life more difficult

fairness (FAHR-nuhss) when one person or group isn't favored over another

gender stereotypes (JEN-duhr STIHR-ee-uh-types) unfair opinions about people based on their sexual identity

injustice (in-JUH-stuhss) unfair treatment

justice (JUH-stuhss) fair treatment

opportunities (ah-puhr-TOO-nuh-teez) chances to do or achieve something

prejudiced (PREH-juh-duhst) judging a person or group without knowing them

stereotype (STIHR-ee-uh-type) an unfair opinion based on one characteristic of a person or group

FIND OUT MORE

WEBSITES

Learning for Justice Classroom Resources—Students texts, tasks, and more
https://www.learningforjustice.org/classroom-resources

Learning for Justice—Learn more about anti-bias work and find the full Social Justice Standards framework
https://www.learningforjustice.org

Social Justice Books—Booklists and a guide for selecting anti-bias children's books
https://socialjusticebooks.org

Welcoming Schools—Creating safe and welcoming schools
https://www.welcomingschools.org

INDEX

ABOUT THE AUTHOR

Emily Chiariello is an anti-bias educator, educational consultant, and former classroom teacher. She is the principal author of the Learning for Justice Social Justice Standards. Emily lives in Buffalo, New York.